Black Umbrella

Also by Katherine Lawrence

Never Mind

June 14/22

Grant — h friendly

t admiration —

Katherine

Black Umbrella

Katherine Lawrence

TURNSTONE PRESS

Turnstone Press gratefully acknowledges the assistance of the Canada Council
for the Arts, the Manitoba Arts Council, the Government of Canada through the
Canada Book Fund, and the Province of Manitoba through the Book Publishing
Tax Credit and the Book Publisher Marketing Assistance Program.

Cover: Melissa Morrow

Cover image: Blood Moon linocut by Angie and Michelle Dreher,
www.twotonepress.com

Printed and bound in Canada.

Library and Archives Canada Cataloguing in Publication

Title: Black umbrella / Katherine Lawrence.
Names: Lawrence, Katherine, 1955- author.
Description: Poems.
Identifiers: Canadiana (print) 20220168342 | Canadiana (ebook) 20220168377 |
    ISBN 9780888017475 (softcover) | ISBN 9780888017482 (EPUB) |
    ISBN 9780888017499 (PDF)
Classification: LCC PS8573.A91135 B53 2022 | DDC C811/.6—dc23

MANITOBA ARTS COUNCIL
CONSEIL DES ARTS DU MANITOBA

Canada Council Conseil des arts
for the Arts   du Canada

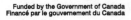

Funded by the Government of Canada
Financé par le gouvernement du Canada

Canada

Manitoba

For my sister

Contents

Vows and Curses

Hooked / 5
My Beautiful Mother / 6
Liminal / 9
Ferus / 21
Up and Away / 23
Nothing Grimm / 25
Vows and Curses / 29
In Over My Head / 31
The Wishful Thinking of a Mall Rat / 32
It's Not Fair to Compare So Let's / 33
The Heart Wants / 35
Love and War / 36

Red Plaid Blanket

I Have Nothing to Wear / 39
Wire Halo Askew / 40
Still Life Inside the Domestic Triangle / 41
Blue Distance / 44
Welcome Aboard / 48
Paper to Pearls / 50
On the Horizon / 51
I Am the Empty Nest / 60
Crimson Scarlet Cardinal Rose / 62
Camel-Wool Coat / 63
Can't Get the Smell of Smoke Out of My Hair / 65
Keeping Mum / 67
Left Behind / 68

Two-Minute Eulogy / 69
The Bitter End / 71
Red Plaid Blanket / 73
Black Umbrella / 74

An Early Evening Hour Inside Out

All My Questions Kneel Down / 77
Latitude / 80
That First Killing Frost of the Season / 82
An Early Evening Hour Inside Out / 84
Bus #12, Saskatoon to Amsterdam / 86
The Modern Woman's Guide to Aging / 88
Name in the Dark / 90
Primary Colours / 91

Notes / 95
Acknowledgements / 97

To go from whitewater rivers' valleys or
from the escarpment to
live on the Saskatchewan prairie is
choosing to find out that
space calls, to a reshaping
of person. This is above and
beyond the going to, the choosing.

—Margaret Avison, "Prairie Poem"

Black Umbrella

Vows and Curses

Hooked

I knew every charm on her bracelet, the silver
sound that chimed as she moved from room
to room. Knew what my father didn't know.

Knew the link between the tiny telephone
dangling from her wrist and the one fixed
to the kitchen wall. It rang once every night

after dinner, a code she translated by touch, her
fingers deciphering the trinket soldered between
a jewel-eyed kitten and the teardrop birthstone.

I pestered her like a child, begged, *Tell me, tell
me, tell me, I can keep a secret,* and I did, or even
better, I forgot. Until I remembered. Years later,

I lifted the lid of a velvet-lined box, uncovered
the bracelet, a piece Little Sister didn't fancy.
Neither did I. What are daughters to do with a

mother's tangle of necklaces, earrings, brooches?
We sorted, donated. Kept an occasional piece
to wear on occasion, fasten a silver chain

to the underside of a veined wrist, listen to her
charms. The way I pretended a stranger dialled
the same wrong number, night after night.

My Beautiful Mother

I colour with orange crayon, try to copy the picture I see in
my head. I have to keep my hands busy while I wait.
Mr. Whealer sits behind his wooden desk, front of the room,
marking arithmetic tests. He doesn't look worried that my
mother is late.

A monarch butterfly once confused me for a flower. I held
my breath until it fluttered from the back of my hand to find
a real, true flower, not a girl at a park in a petunia-pink
sundress. I switch crayons, trace a waxy black vein outside
and across the teardrop shapes. My mother is never on time.
I'd like to turn around in my desk, show my scribbles to
Debbie—but she left after the bell rang with everybody else.

Mr. Whealer is the first male teacher I've had in my life.
The only man in the school except for the principal. And
the janitor. I wish I had the nerve to ask the janitor how
he lost the thumb on his left hand. A small, knuckled
stump. I bow my head whenever the janitor sweeps past
me in the hall, lower my eyes. I don't want him to catch
me staring.

My mother flashed a photograph of me asleep in bed
sucking my thumb. She waved the black-and-white at me,
proof she was right. I didn't believe I sucked my thumb,
only babies suck their thumbs. Not a Grade 4 girl.
Sometimes I have to fight not to lift my thumb to my
mouth. I've seen the janitor bring that small stump to his
lips, whisk his hand away. He misses his missing thumb.

I hear the *click, click, click* of high heels announcing themselves against a hard linoleum shine dulled and restored every day. Mr. Whealer rises to his feet as my mother pauses slender as a comma inside the doorframe. His eyes widen, and for a brief moment I see what he sees. A woman posing in black heels polished to Crayola brilliance. Long silky legs disappearing beneath the navy-blue hem of a trench coat belted tight at the waist, long sleeves, the collar turned up. Her wide smile, white, straight teeth, big hazel eyes, black hair styled by the hairdresser she visits every Wednesday. Nardina. Oh man, how could I forget? She's late for the parent-teacher-student interview because she's just come from the beauty salon.

Long after I've had daughters of my own, long after I learn how to draw boundaries around the men in my mother's life, the men who looked, the men who phoned, the men who followed, I will continue to wonder if she drove below the speed limit that day, lingered at stop signs, calculated her entrance to arrive at the weekday height of her uncommon beauty, her coat belt cinched tighter than required for a run-of-the-mill trip to the bank, the grocery store, my swim lessons. Or maybe the entrance was for me. Maybe I was supposed to watch, observe, appreciate the lessons she gave me at home. How to walk, turn, smile. Not slump, complain, suck my thumb.

Mr. Whealer doesn't look away. Dark shoes, coat, hair, the long line of brass buttons, the singular touch of deep pink on her lips, a faint blush rising to her cheeks as she lets him, invites him to take his time.

He coughs into his fist, seems to remember why my mother is here. He offers her an adult-sized chair brought in from the staff room for the interviews taking place all week. I move from my desk to stand beside her, inhale her hairspray, let the sweet florals catch the back of my throat. I edge closer, my nose a breath away from the side of her powdered face. She's mine. She belongs to me, Little Sister, and our father.

I hear what I know. I am a polite girl who achieves good grades, excels at reading, spelling, composition. I participate in class. I am kind, respectful, punctual. And something else: Mr. Whealer suggests I need extra help with long division but his words fly fast, like the numbers I can't hold in my head. He rolls a pen between his fingers, his eyes grading my mother. A for long legs, A+ for pointed breasts, A++ for the pulse at the base of her throat, her full lips, her bright eyes as she accepts the pen he offers.

I try to insert myself as the subject of today's meeting but they've moved to a place I can't reach. Worse, I've lost her scent to something animal, something not-my-mother, her pupils glowing inky black as the signature she scratches on the back of my report card.

Liminal

1.

Little Sister and me. What's left of the day is ours.
We play blonde, brunette, redhead. Unpack vacant
eyes, bullet breasts, stiff arms, pull apart legs. The
flat-footed man-doll stares above the backcombed,
the curled, the teased. Little Sister is eight coming
nine. I am twelve. My blood already begun. Too old
for these bloodless bodies. Almost.

Peculiar we played on the gold carpeted landing,
above the bedroom stairs. Peculiar, given all the
rooms and windows. The split-level house. Windows
filled with late-afternoon winter sun, windows framed
by lined curtains, sheers, blinds. Peculiar we chose the
only windowless space in the house. An in-between
place, a liminal space. Toys not allowed to loiter.
Pick up, clean up, put away after play.

We squat like small animals, ears alert, black
lidless eyes at the back of our brushed and combed
heads. Six carpeted steps away from the pork chops
our mother unwraps, pounds flat, flips over. The hot
fat and salt of her. The sizzle, the fry. The wall phone.
Her voice and the long beige tail she drags to the milk-
white fridge, electric white stove, double window above
the stainless-steel sink. Chrome faucets turning hot,
cold. My ears tuned to sound waves under water. Warm
tones dripping from Mother's voice. Her special friend.
The secret chews my nails, bites my lower lip, itches
behind my knees, the skin scratched raw. Little Sister

doesn't know. Our Dad doesn't know. Cannot. Not
ever. *Promise?* I promise.

Buttons the size of a sparrow's eye. Tiny shoes lost
in the silky folds of an emerald-green ballgown.
Or inside Little Sister's mouth. She doesn't swallow.
Sucks each shoe like a Chiclet, one plastic stiletto
at a time. Spits into her sweater cuff, dries the shoe, fits
a tiny pointed foot. A very Prince Charming performance.
My every eye on her in case she chokes.

We jazz skinny dolls in tight capri pants, sequined
dresses. Pink bikini under a ballgown for the swimwear
scene switch. Dolls on the beach. The French Riviera.
Carpeted gold sand.

2.

Our mother changes with both fashion seasons. Spring
and fall. She's a model, a slim, tall quick-change artist.
Strides down, across, back and up along T-shaped, curtained
catwalks. Shows lingerie, couturier daywear, evening wear,
ready-to-wear. Furs (mink, beaver, red fox), kid-leather gloves
long as stockings, high heels, flats, slingbacks, hats, handbags,
shoulder bags, beaded clutch bags. Pause, pose, a theatrical
turn. Her fashion photos in women's magazines, Eaton's
catalogue, the local newspaper. Clipped, filed. Our mother,
her other life.

3.

The telephone rings as we play, calls her mind away
from its slow simmer. Fashion shows and fitting dates,
time, place. Her appointment book stroked like a black
cat allowed on the kitchen counter.

4.

I make my bed every morning before school plus Saturday,
Sunday, Christmas Day, summer holidays. Straighten
my bedspread, the quilted pastel blue poppies, each flower
large as a dinner plate. Sometimes the bed looks like I slept
in it. Mother shows me again and again. How to place thumb
and forefinger on the red stitch she threaded to the top-centre
edge of the bedspread. *See?* Tuck sheets, blankets, pull
the cover up and over the pillow. *No, not the same hand.*
The other hand. Use both hands. Use your head. Think.

In science class, I think about tectonic plates, oceanic plates.
Mr. Brown hands us fresh mimeographed maps. The pale
blue ink smells like white sugar. We trace a path along the
Pacific Ocean. First in pencil, then in red to show the Ring
of Fire. We open notebooks, switch to pen as he dictates:
the long horseshoe-shaped seismically active belt of
earthquake epicentres ... He spells *seismically.* He spells
epicentre. He says tremors uproot trees, turn mountains
into rubble, shake families from their beds.

5.

A Japanese schoolgirl visits my dreams. She reads under
her desk by day. By night, she sleeps on top of her bedspread,
eyes open, arms crossed over her flat chest, fully dressed in
jeans and shirt beneath a pink silk kimono. When the earth
sends up the first tremors, she will leap from bed, wake her
parents, her little sister, grab the cat by its belled collar.
Run.

Where? I don't know where the Japanese schoolgirl runs.
I lose her in my dark. All I see is her narrow bed, the smooth
Pacific-blue cover. Untouched. As if nothing happened.

6.

Dad is a salesman. He sells bandages, ointments, rolls
of skin-coloured gauze, golden shampoo for babies.
The shampoo promises no more tears. Imagine.
Our bathroom cupboard shelves look and smell like the
pharmacy counter in a drugstore.

He travels every week, a black book in the glove box. Meal
expenses, motel costs, gas, customer names, addresses, phone
numbers. His territory. Our dad has his own territory.

Suit pockets full of pink and green dinner mints for Little
Sister and me. His briefcase downstairs at night, the dull metal
office desk in the basement, white shirtsleeves rolled above
his elbows, head bent, the gooseneck lamp spilling light
across catalogues, receipts, sales order forms, the wicker
wastebasket under the desk filled with crumpled black carbon
sheets. Inky imprint on his fingers, pale grey residue under
his nails. Come morning, he showers, shaves. Dark suit, fresh
white shirt, silver cufflinks, spiced cologne, striped tie knotted
at his throat.

7.

My place in the family Ford is the backseat on Dad's side.
Little Sister sits between him and Mother. If I close my eyes,
I can see behind my spine, penetrate the padded grey vinyl
upholstery, the coiled springs, peer into the airless dark:
spare tire, snow shovel, road flares, jumper cables, red plaid
blanket, focus until I find the white moulded plastic kit,
a red cross on duty, medical scissors, gauze pads, triangular
bandages, dressings for cuts, gashes, gouges, wounds.

8.

Black leather flats, legs long as her climb up the gold
carpeted stairs. How did I not hear her step, step, step,
turn, step, pause, pose, chin down. Her static pose.

Girls. I look up, stand up. Little Sister shadows me.
Mother's brown eyes, dark, thick lashes, black hair cut
chin-length, backcombed, sprayed. Her scent a long-
stemmed rose, red lipstick. Never wears lipstick unless
errands, appointments, a visitor. We don't see visitors
before dinner on a school night.

One slender hand on the banister as if she might tip
over. I love that hand. I love both those hands. I love
the veins on the right hand, the puffy blue-grey letter *H*
for Helen. Monogrammed and manicured.

What if she falls?

9.

Tonight, after dinner, your father and I plan to tell you
that we intend to separate. Twist, turn, freeze—*Understand?*
How do I already know?

Tectonic plates grind past one another in opposite directions.
Bonus question for ten marks. The North American Plate.
The Pacific Plate. The bread-and-butter plate smashed
on the kitchen floor. Bare feet, jigsaw shards same shade
of beige as the no-wax vinyl. Blood and a Band-Aid
I tear open by pulling the single red thread along the fold.

A smile on her face. Not in her voice. *Your father or*
with me.

10.

A piece inside my head flies to the lakeshore, a restaurant
my grandparents choose for birthdays, their anniversary,
Easter lunch. How do I answer the waitress in the black
dress uniform, white apron snugged at the waist? I can do
this. What do I say when she asks apple juice or tomato; rice,
baked potato, French fries? I can do this. Or later, our polished
plates shining with buttery fat. She swings back, clears
the table, poses the final question: strawberry, vanilla, or
chocolate?

Demand a menu, throw a tantrum, kick the waitress, pitch
a milk glass at the picture window. Best view in the house.

11.

You.

Nothing moves. Not the late-afternoon amber light, not
the gold twist fibres under my bare feet, not the air
in my lungs.

A moist hand slips into mine. *I'll go wherever Kath goes.*

Good. Mother lifts her hand from the banister, her balance
recovered. She looks from me to the confusion of naked
breasts, half-dressed torsos, twisted heads, miniature sweaters,
dresses, skirts, bathing suits, hairbrushes, combs, a black
tuxedo.

I drop Little Sister's hand, kneel near the doll trunk. Gather,
fold, cram, crush, bury the mess.

Ferus

A plum tree in the backyard? Wooden swing? Broken gate?
I recall the skin, lips, and tongue, dark gold flesh, honeyed
spit rivering my wrists.

Not the tree.　　My legs, limbs, bare feet jiving the sky.
Not the swing.　　My wild blood. The unhinged gate.

　　I did not want to leave the woods.
　　I did not want to bathe or eat with a fork.

Blackberries, raspberries, gooseberries, mint, morel
mushrooms, sweet ramps, cress, creeks
to cup an addict's thirst.

　　I did not wish my tumble tamed.
　　I did not muster to any call, but One.

　　I love the dark hours of my being
　　in which my senses drop into the deep.

Stopped me in mid-fright. Mother, patrolling the ravine
after dark with flashlight and rope.

　　Slip-knotted me at the intersection of black bear and
　　squirrel. Pulled tight. Dragged me up from animal
　　to muddy poppet. Scrubbed my private stink, my rank
　　air, my mineral muck. Kettle and scolded.

Rough-towelled my essence. Stuffed
my legs into white leotards. Banded my torso
in a collared dress that choked my spoke.

Starched me.

> A magic doorstop, a big mother-of-pearl seashell that
> I recognized as a messenger from near and far
> because I could hold it to my ear—when nobody was
> there to stop me—and discover the tremendous
> pounding of my own blood, and of the sea.

Months and months of Novembers.

The sky in a sunken mood.

I'd been on my way.
I was on the cusp of becoming

      something   some   thing
      other than her.

Up and Away

I carry fourteen saved dollars folded
inside a brown leather shoulder purse
pressed against my hip like an amulet.

I do not know the word *amulet*. I know

not to lose Little Sister in the wool-coated,
overheated crowd. She holds my hand
as we push past a miniature village, tiny
mechanical girls and boys skating circles
on mirrored glass trimmed with snow
sprayed from a can. We ride the up

escalator to the top floor for a better view,
eight life-sized reindeer in mid-flight,
Rudolph's red nose a neon bulb Little Sister
believes will guide the sleigh as she sleeps
all night while I listen in the dark
to Santa and his wife playing pickup sticks
with a broken marriage.

We buy English toffee for our grandfather.
We buy boxed stationary for our grandmother.
We buy perfumed bubble bath for our mother.
We buy soap-on-a-rope for our father.

We buy chocolate-covered cinnamon hearts
for the bus ride home to 36 Price Avenue,
the split-level our parents will divide, sell
after the snowman on our front lawn melts,
his stone eyes returned to mineral matter.

I wish now I had gift-wrapped my brown leather
purse for Little Sister. I wish I had adjusted
the strap across her narrow shoulders, shown her
how to walk with confidence, the purse secured
at her hip. How to run, no—fly as far away
from home as I did.

Nothing Grimm

1.

We moved into a two-bedroom apartment, the ceilings
stippled with white plaster and glitter. Nights alone I
babysat while Mother took classes or dated a man
with no last name, a man whose plans were unreliable
as Mother's moods. She blamed his wife.

I let Little Sister jump giggly on the bed, arms overhead,
fingertips reaching for sparkle. She believed things had
gotten better. I'd read her a bedtime story, nothing Grimm.
Tuck her in, try my hand at high school French, math, my
concentration shot with black holes. Instead, I dreamed,
pages and pages. About what? A tree house, the laddered
height, a room with desk, chair, lantern, a bedroll to unroll
my red-lily rage. A top bunk for Little Sister.

2.

Mother vowed flat stomach, hips, thighs, comely ass. Broke
the nightly fast with Florida grapefruit sliced pink, half-cup
mild curd, coffee black. High noon dropped dry wafers
round as moons on a bread plate. Late afters, Scotch and
water costumed in a child's yellow tumbler. Hail merry full
of smoke. She tithed coins, crystal, a sable mink coat.
Placed her faith in Estée, Chanel, Elizabeth, L'Oréal. Never
gained a pound, never confessed the banker, the lawyer,
the radio man. Men who wore gold wedding rings. Men
we kept secret from our father when we visited him
in another apartment, a one-bedroom he furnished with
a secondhand couch, Grandmother's picnic plates stacked
in the cupboard. And in the coat closet, twin rollaway cots,
beds that folded up in the middle like two hands pressed
together in prayer.

3.

A dream returns. Little Sister is driving a car while I
scissor her long black braid with a pair of sewing
shears. She rolls down the window, lets the lopped hair
fly. The wheels hit gravel, skid. I scream, *Slow down,
steer with both hands on your own fucking trauma!* She
pulls into a field, cuts the engine, kills the brights.
The roof hums open. We tip back our heads. She looks
like my twin. *Better to see the starlit whatnot,* she says,
swanning her skinny neck. The sex-call of crickets
frills the air, countless oracles all speaking at once.

4.

I will always be sorry for yelling at Little Sister. Me,
her unpaid babysitter. But once she starts wearing a bra
and shaving her legs, I let her root through my suede leather
shoulder bag for cigarettes, borrow my patched jeans, paw
the stinking black sweaters heaped in the laundry, abuse tiny
pots of charcoal eyeshadow junked on my dresser, wave
a mascara wand through her dark lashes, drag an ebony line
under her eyelids, don my blackest clothes, smoke, drink, roll
a joint, go numb, slip away past midnight.

Vows and Curses

1.

We attend our father's wedding
as spectators stunned into silence,
the ceremony performed by actors
who follow a script understood
by everyone in the church except us.
We sit when we should kneel, stand
too late, stand too soon, open the wrong
book, miss the first verse, don't know
where to look when the groom in his
dark suit turns to the bride, smiles
into her eyes, kisses her upturned face.

We are no longer children yet we trip
from the pew, stumble in the recessional
line behind the groom and bride, past
strangers to the left, old cousins on the
right, file in slow motion toward dark
wooden doors open wide to the chill,
late-afternoon snow falling like confetti.
I button my coat, move down the steps,
no turning back, no more silly fantasies.
Our father has taken a new woman, a fine
woman, to be his wife. Her parents speak
Italian to her, English to my father, kiss
him on both cheeks. I shiver on the church
sidewalk, throw a few grains of white rice
at my father's happy ending.

2.

My high school boyfriend picks me up in his
blue Volkswagen after the dinner. Little Sister
catches a lift home with the newlyweds en route
to their honeymoon hotel. The bride sends us off
with wedding favours. Plus one extra.

What did Mother do once we were home in bed?
I still hear water running in the sink as she washes
the day's dishes, see the bottle of red wine beside
a small pink pouch on the kitchen table. She sits,
tops up her drink, fingers the gift filled with sugar-
coated almonds, a traditional Italian wedding treat
said to symbolize the bittersweetness of marriage.
What did she think as she sat alone? Perhaps of
her ex, cursing his happiness. Perhaps of her wedding,
twenty-one years earlier, cursing her own stupidity.
Perhaps she swore never to marry again. If so, she
stayed true to her word. What I know with the certainty
of morning is this: she drained the bottle, turned her
mind to the satin pouch, untied the treat, lifted a candy
to her lips, tongue, teeth, bit down hard, winced in pain.
A back tooth. Cracked. *Damn him, damn them both to hell.*

In Over My Head

My difficult truth
resorts to methods
found in the Old
Testament, delivering
a dream to my numb,
drunk teen self,
images that drench me
in sweat. I shiver
unholy cold, haunted
by Mother's eyes,
her head underwater,
my heart-thumping
race from shore to the
middle of a midnight-
black lake, my arms,
her arms flailing,
naked. She grabs
my shoulders, forces
me down. I twist, buck,
kick free, gasp air,
wake to face a vision
that feels like gospel
prophecy: I cannot save
my beautiful mother.

The Wishful Thinking of a Mall Rat
from journal notes circa 1974

If I slip through the sliding glass doors.
If I locate the shop Viviane owns in the mall.
If I wait at the sales counter while she assists a girl
and a mother.
If I hear her ask the customer if payment will be cheque
or cash.
If I turn my face to hers.
If I give her a moment to recognize me.
If I nod yes, I need help.
If I let her choose a dress for my high school grad.
If I follow her to the curtained change room.
If I invite her to look at me in the full-length mirror.
If I show her that everything I try is too big, too ill-fitting.
If I beg her to see that I can't wear the secret
by myself anymore.
If I speak her husband's name. Out loud.
If I speak my mother is the other woman.
If I listen to her say she knows my mother's name,
knows who I am, sees me in the mall skipping class.
If I cry, sob in childish self-pity, would this unlikely
ally hang my pain on the same rack as her betrayal?

It's Not Fair to Compare So Let's

a)

My roommate's mother rides a Greyhound bus
for eight hours, then grabs a cab to our basement
apartment off campus. Her weekend luggage
is a soft-sided dull brown suitcase and a cardboard
box loaded with fall market fruit. She unpacks ripe
red apples, green pears, dark purple Concord grapes,
peaches firm as tennis balls, each piece washed,
rinsed. And more gifts: white cotton-lace camisoles.
One for Laura, one for me. Laura offers her bed
but this mother opts for the pull-out couch instead.
That night, she treats us to pork cutlets at a diner
downtown. She doesn't backcomb her thin grey hair,
or wear foundation to hide wrinkles that soften
as she shares stories from home about Laura's father,
Laura's three older brothers. We leave together,
I hang back a few paces, let them chat, hold hands,
follow the long scenic route home, the floodlit Rideau
Canal that will soon freeze for skating miles and miles.

b)

My mother hits town that same first semester in a navy-
blue Lincoln Continental driven by a married man
whose other life is a wife and two little kids.
He and Mother show up at the apartment after checking
in at a historic hotel that costs as much for two nights
as all my textbooks for the year. He carries one bag,
a black leather hard-shell portable bar the size of a
Smith Corona typewriter case. Mother unsnaps the brass
locks, sets up cocktail hour beside the two-burner hot
plate. Martini glasses, shaker, vodka, dry vermouth,
olives. Yes, I have ice. No, thank you. Laura escapes
to the library. I sip cold tea. Mother tells me again I'm
just like my father. Dull, no fun. I don't argue, push back,
speak up. Someone in this party for three needs to stay
sober, not lose the keys.

The Heart Wants

I am nineteen when I meet him,
twenty-nine when I finally agree he's
right. What kind of man waits a decade
for a woman? I don't know. Wait,

that's a lie. The better question is this:
what took me so long? I was more rabbit
than girl in those days, small game
sensing danger, twitches its ears, sniffs

the air, bolts. My knack for survival born
of a mother who assumed I'd fall for the same
trap. She warned me, packed me off with
a flashlight, a kiss, and direction.

Earn your own gold, she told me. I travelled
both poles, trekked alone to better, harder jobs
while he wrote letters, phoned me long distance,
a friend who dialled into the heart of the matter.

What was the matter? Not a thing. I needed time.
Time to fall in love with my body, my voice, my
brave, surefooted, animal self.

Love and War

We opt for a civil ceremony
on neutral soil, the prairie,
my home away, a giddy,
wild spring wind, two gold
rings. My mother books Air
Canada, arrives from the east
wearing her best behaviour.
My father and his wife plead busy
lives, excuses, excuses. He's
unwilling to declare peace
on a morning in May, meet
my western in-laws, shake
hands with my new husband,
join our small party for lunch
in a private room at an airport
hotel, break bread with his ex.

Red Plaid Blanket

I Have Nothing to Wear

What is the dress code for motherhood? * Where among the black tie, smart casual, formal, business casual, no-shirt-no-shoes-no-service, is the instruction for how to dress for motherhood? * Why didn't Coco design the little black wash-and-wear motherhood dress? * Perhaps motherhood suggests garments with hoods, such as the black leather draped over a hawk's head by its human captor. * Then again, why doesn't motherhood come with a signature colour like army green, hospital green, camo? * Why does most every job, except motherhood, arrive with a uniform? * Might a uniform correct the perception that motherhood is child's play? * Is it true or false that joy requires a padded hanger to maintain its full-bodied shape? * What are the telltale signs of motherhood? * When did the apron seize your attention? * How does one accessorize for motherhood? * What about footwear? * What about deep, functional pockets? * Ever heard of a coatigan? * How about an updo and rhinestone earrings for those down days when motherhood needs a touch of glam?

Wire Halo Askew

Dust sugars the shoulders of Mary, Joseph, three wooden
magi in a manger on my mantle. So answer me, wise people:
where might we bed my unexpected guest? Aunt Clarisse
will fly tonight across tundra, lakes, boreal forest, prairie,
touch down at our house, come undone. No room, no food at
the inn full of daughters home for the holidays with
boyfriends who eat like goats. 'Tis the season for losing
luggage and good reason. Aunt is too frail for holiday travel
yet she insists: wheelchair, cane, oxygen, medication. Aisle
seat in first class. We sweep and dust, launder, sprinkle
lavender. Decorate, adorn, bedeck. What the heck. Hunt for
another box inside a bigger box shelved behind, tucked away
slapdash, slipshod, a crochet angel, wire halo askew, her mouth
a torn red vowel O, O, O, thread and needle to the rescue. A
single stitch. In time and out of butter. Dear oh dear. So much
is dear this time of year. A good night's rest, yes, yes. To the
matter of a manger. Where to bed Aunt Clarisse? Her heart
palpitations migrate across her chest like caribou thundering
north. Or so she says. The weak, the sick left behind. Not her.
Short life? Shortbread. 350°F, ten to twelve minutes until
golden. A blue glazed bowl brimming with clementines next to
the bed one of us will give up, give
over—the gift. She is to us.

Still Life Inside the Domestic Triangle
after attending a retrospective of Mary Pratt (1935-2018)

1.

Sable brushes, oil on canvas, linen, the surface
of all things a still life. Mary paints *Red Currant Jelly,*
apples, bananas, pudding, trout. She paints *June Geranium,*
the cuttings in a clear glass vase. Waterline, sightline,
the scent of chocolate cake, grilled salmon, wild violets,
house on fire, *Donna* the other woman on his fingers at dusk,
evening's catch gutted clean, the air redolent. Sable brush
potent as a pig's snout, *Girl in a Wicker Chair.*

2.

I stroll the gallery, listen to colour. Subtext burdens the still
life. *Dishcloth on Line #1, #2, #3, #4.* A married woman
considers a triangle while ironing a basket of shirts, table-
cloth, handkerchiefs. One side of the iron for each person
in her marriage. She presses his collar, steam hisses, rises.
Elemental. *Girl in My Dressing Gown,* fabric unfolding.

3.

I return to the exhibition a third time, study *The Bed*. Empty,
unmade. Sheets cooling. I recall another woman in bed with a
married man, the oldest trope in the world. He wakes, thinks
about his wife. He steps into the bathroom. The woman listens
with her eyes closed. Her shoulders bare. Hears the sound of
a man rearranging his life while shaving. He cuts his chin. *Girl
in Glitz*, infidelity suggested by angle, slope, curve, waist, hip,
thigh. *It is difficult to paint a person if that person is looking
out of the painting* ....

4.

Why did he choose his wife instead of his lover? I will
always wonder. *Dinner for One*, leftovers, yesterday's salad.
A bowl of fruit.

5.

The man is a lifelong student of World War II. Home in time
for dinner, *Silver Fish on Crimson Foil*. She knows. *The
Dining Room with a Red Rug*. He missed the long, quiet
nights at home with his own war.

6.

Mary writes, *I was touched by the marks of the buttons on*
her stomach and the impressions of stitches and zipper left by
her jeans.

Frame, wire, nail. The other woman drives him to the airport,
drops him off at Arrivals and Departures, kisses the bead of
dark dried blood on his chin. She has saved the expense
of parking and other costs, greater costs, personal. She returns
home to her one-bedroom apartment, unlocks the door, steps
into her still life. Oval braided rug, corduroy couch, hassock,
tempered-glass coffee table. *Pomegranates in a Crystal Bowl*,
jewelled reds shattered and reflected from one intricate
surface to another.

Blue Distance

A boyish waiter in mirrored sunglasses adjusts the angle
of our turquoise patio umbrella. Cuts the high-noon glare
without cropping the lake view. Good table.

Ladies care for a drink? My jaw joints go rigid. I need
this guy to look at me, not my seventy-year-old mother,
but I can't see his shaded eyes. *I'd love a gin and tonic,*
she says. *Think fast,* I tell myself. *Make that two
cranberry spritzers. Please.*

In four hours, a return ticket will fly me home, 3,000 km west
of the Toronto skyline. The Prairies. A world away from the
chain of freshwater lakes I memorized as a kid. I test myself,
recover the old mnemonic SHO ME: Superior, Huron,
Ontario, Michigan, Erie. I wonder if my own kids, both
in high school, would pass the same test.

A light breeze tangles the windward side of my mother's
chin-length, dyed hair. She doesn't fight back, finger-comb.
She's turned her attention to the sailboats tacking across the
blue distance. A race. I know better than to comment. Single
mast, two-person daysailers are roped to my father. Luxury
yachts remain anchored to the other man, the big talker
who never left his wife, never intended to leave his wife,
his kids.

Drinks arrive, sweating. Three parts mineral water, one
part cranberry, an orange slice. I don't know if my mother
is savvy to my strategy but my defense is ready. She'll drive
home to her apartment along one of the busiest highways
in North America. She might believe I'm thinking of her
safety. She'd be half right.

The wind on the lake shifts again. I see my adolescent self
in a neon orange life jacket, two hands gripping the jib sheet,
eyes on the trim, yanking hard, letting off, acting fast when
my dad shouts from behind the wooden rudder, *Jibe ho!*
Watch your head.

I need a clear head. I study the lunch menu, ask if she feels
hungry. She diets. I know there's nothing in her stomach
except strong black coffee, a slice of toast spread with sugar-
free, seedless strawberry jam.

I suppose you ordered room service for breakfast, she says.
Translation: you think you're smart.

I've been in Toronto for a week, split my time between
a conference, a night with my father and his wife, another
with my mother, my sister, my brother-in-law, escaped
for a weekend getaway with old pals. I only share drinks
with my husband and friends. Giddy tipplers.

She chooses the Asian salad. *You love cilantro?* I ask.
I'll join you. We close our menus. She tells me some people
insist the herb tastes like soap. Not us. She smiles at me.
I have never seen my mother in public without lipstick.
Today she wears girly pink. She stirs her drink with a plastic
straw. I bow my head, pretend to smooth the cloth napkin
spread across my lap, offer silent prayer to Chinese parsley,
the love-or-hate herb.

Two ounces of gin in her drink and she'd tell me I'd look
younger if I wore makeup. Four ounces, I become a fool
for letting my hair go grey, six and I'm dull, boring as my
father. Instead, she sips diluted fruit juice and shares her
method for washing, storing fresh herbs. I hear the ice
in my drink clink as it melts. She insists the trick is to cut
greens using herb scissors.

You own more scissors than the Queen, I say. She raises
her glass. I join her in a salute to essential tools. Grape
shears, pinking shears, her black-handled sewing scissors,
craft scissors, hair scissors, cuticle trimmers. Fourteen?
Twenty? She promises to count when she gets home, phone
me tomorrow with the number.

Translation: she intends for us to remain talking.

I give the waiter our order. She doesn't interrupt, demand
dressing on the side, rice instead of noodles, no chicken, no
peanuts. I love her when she's kind. To herself, to me,
to the waiter, to my sister, to the few friends in her life.

I've got an early birthday present for you, I say.

My leather bag sits slumped at my feet. I reach down,
retrieve a small cardboard box, pass the gift across the table.

Her face flushes, not from the June sun but from a surprise
that unfolds in plain view of patio guests who hear our
laughter, glance our way. She is on display. A woman
out for lunch with another woman whose olive skin, round
eyes, black lashes, straight nose, and thick hair match her
own. As a child, I was told that I looked like my mother.
As a teen, I was told we looked like sisters. As a middle-aged
woman whose dark brown hair is streaked with silver-grey,
I've been asked which one of us is the daughter. Who is
the mother?

My mind shoots a dozen pictures of her as she sits taller,
prouder, in a pale blue, loose-fitting shirt-dress, a forgiving
style. She opens the small box, sets down the lid, unfolds
the white tissue paper, accepts help from a breeze.

You shouldn't spend your money on me.
Translation: I'm thrilled you spend your money on me.

She lifts a necklace from a nest of jewellers' wool, dangles
a sterling silver egg-shaped pendant in the air between us.
It sways like a plumb bob, sparkles in the sunlight.

Welcome Aboard

I buy silk scarves, sun hats, sleeveless dresses,
gowns, a pair of green sequined capris and a black

strappy bathing suit to fool myself into believing
that if I look the part, I won't fall apart

during the impending shipwreck of a family holiday—
seven nights all aboard Legend of the Seas,

a tower of staterooms, dining rooms, pools, casinos,
movie theatres, miniature golf floating above

the underworld. I need armour to survive my father's
eighth decade under the sun, a celebration

of the family King Neptune glued together with spit
and a second wife. The truth is I'm seasick

from a lifetime of slamming doors and pulling hair,
the ocean floor heaving. Times like this I miss

my mother, queen of troubled seas, because she always
knew what to wear, what to say, what not to say,

and said it anyway, but she jumped ship years ago, now
lives alone with a cat and a bottomless bottle of Seagram's

Seven. Do I need a drink? No, I need to give this holiday
a chance, play shuffleboard, overeat, burn the tops

of my feet, dance with the king, kiss him goodnight, then
stroll the upper deck alone in gratitude, count my lucky

stars for a lifetime of riding the high seas with my father
at the helm, standing firm.

Paper to Pearls

We've shared the same bed for thirty years, created
two daughters, adopted a yellow dog, saved coins
in a tin bucket full of holes stuffed with long hours
and freelance jobs that kept us driving through rush hour
every day, every month, year after year, and home again
to dinner at a table crammed with plates, forks, fingers,
tongues, and buttered grins.

How tall the crooked tower of dirty dishes, pots sticky
with rice and green vegetables. Did we talk about anything
in those years other than what was or wasn't in the fridge,
the gas tank, the chequing account? Did we say goodnight?
Did we kiss before we fell asleep? Did I sleep?

Or did I swim in and out of those nights, surfacing at the
sounds of my life, the cough and cry from beds across the hall,
my nightgown's thin hem rushing the wooden floor,
cool tap water running to overflow a child's plastic cup.

When darkness settles the covers around my bare shoulders,
I lie awake beside you, spooning your heat, wondering about
the mystery that led me here, to you and all that we built
with our beautiful bodies, all those decades ago. How quiet
the nights are now.

On the Horizon

1.

Chemical plumes rise from stacks that pock
the shores of Steeltown, Lunch Bucket Town,
The Hammer, a city that makes me sick
with longing.

I worked downtown, my eyes watering from toxins
in the air. I'd fan my long hair across my mouth, nose,
take shallow breaths, dizzy breaths, hoping to escape
from poisons polluting fish, birds, my lungs. Hoping
to escape from my mother.

I set my sights on clean air, The Prairies. I wanted
a holiday away to refresh my lungs. I didn't plan
to leave home forever, yet here I am, a crone living
in a rectangular province Americans can't pronounce
or locate until I say, *Above North Dakota*.

Here is the church and here is the steeple. Peek
inside and here are my teams: home versus away,
touchdowns for both sides, cheering live from
the radio broadcasting across Canada on a Sunday
afternoon.

I stand at a stove miles and miles from the place
where I was born, a pot on simmer. I hold a wooden
spoon, deglaze fatty bits of chicken, wonder how I might
reduce Canada to a sauce, strain and pour this country
into a gravy boat, climb aboard, sail from Saskatoon to
Hamilton in an afternoon, watch the game on TV with Dad,
then wave, *So long, see you next Sunday,* instead of next
year.

How much time have I spent traversing
Saskatchewan
        Manitoba
                Ontario?

2.

I drive with a visitor's map to the industrial heartland
of Canada, the Golden Horseshoe. Try my luck. I sing
behind the wheel, all the words to *Ontari-ari-ari-o*, pick
up speed along the highway, fix my grip on glimpses
of lake, not river, lake, not slough, pitch my tent on the
geologic core of the continent, hug the deep green boreal
night until the hum of semi-trucks calls me back to the road,
my intention set to reach the lake, see silver dimes sailing
across the years I leaned into the wind as my father's first
mate, safe in a neon orange life jacket.

Now comes the decision: to cross or not to cross the Skyway
Bridge or drive the Lakeshore. Either way I've got multi-
lanes of recall ahead. There's no way to avoid memory's
rush hour, the sub-rosa conspiracy of the psyche, because
I'm home, I'm back in the place I never left even though
my body and its other family—my husband, our daughters—
inhabit an ecozone that sends the western red lily shooting
up like orange flames from tinder-dry prairie ditches, roadside
depressions where the trillium would wither and cry.

Somewhere in a private zone all my own, a flower blooms
the colour of dust. How do I know? Because here everything
holds moisture as I drive the powerful, essential ritual of return.
I park, walk, knock, numb my knuckles against the door
that unhinges me. A gift of lilacs, the mauve hue saturated
violet-blue.

Mother? Are you home?

3.

Where does memory live?
How does my mind confuse a bundle
of wild lilacs wrapped in newsprint
for the cat buried so long ago he's
dust in the perfumed air? I had no
warning, no way to guess the weight
of lilacs carried like a swaddled thing
in my arms might unbalance me. Yet
in a quickening, the poundage settles
into the crook of my elbows, sly
as a butcher's thumb, and I'm weeping
about the cat whose lives survived the
move from house to apartment. Balcony
cat, the cat that never climbed another
tree, never again hunted mice, songbirds,
killed for sport, his green eyes trained
on my sister and me. Those nights
Mother was on the prowl.

4.

The tiny round clock still ticks after all these years,
its face the size of a silver dollar, a gift from her lover

and thank you, no, I don't wish to wake beside a keepsake
of the man who waited in a hotel room while my father

was at work and we were in school, I don't need a reminder
to forgive what I can't forget because my own clock reverts

to the time zone of girlhood as she tries to hand me the clock
like a prize I've won for holding onto the past. *Don't be*

so melodramatic, she says. *It's only a clock.* Always and
forever, her word against mine. She pauses for a vodka

martini, breaks from the endless job of sorting, packing.
I'm here to muscle her into a smaller, cheaper apartment,

her retirement money tight as a banker's smile. She asks
me to join her, mix a drink, be a sport. *One olive or two?*

5.

I tally the price I've paid for driving across time zones,
the cost of a traveller's costume, the price of gifts, the
amount of silver required for round-trip flights that feel
triangular, and now the charge for nursing care. *Bad luck,*
she says. Lung cancer we thought was pneumonia.
The disease a champion that will win before she starts
the fight. I move her again within the year. This time
to my sister's house, the guest room at the top of a circular
staircase. Mother complains the elevated air makes it hard
for her to breathe. We pretend with her until the oxygen
arrives. Metal cannisters, clear plastic tubes, the hissing
sound of anger without the fight.

I keep her company while my sister works. Read, balance
soup on a tray, fetch a blanket, not the pink, not the plaid,
no, she demands blue, the Wallis blue, asks what became
of the key chain she gave me, her favourite words engraved
on a brass tag: *a woman can never be too rich or too thin.*
At long last, she's in a space that lets her believe anything.

6.

We watch a fashion show on TV, vintage hats for antique
heads. I sweater her bosom, pearl her cleavage. Mother's
mood swings up. She applauds, drifts back to sleep. I kiss
her goodnight, goodbye, promise I'll return.

Back at home, away from her twilight, we hatch schemes
by phone. Shorten the hem of our long distance, collapse
then and now, ease ourselves into tomorrow. I dream the
geometry of my mother's body: angle of hands folded
on her lap. My lips pressed against her forehead as I bend
to give.

7.

She counts the peas on her plate.
She shuffles cards for solitaire.
She presses her pen against reason.

Her limbic system has gone giddy.
Her wonder is illuminated.
Her ice bruises when she stirs.

She doesn't eat alone anymore.
She doesn't dress before noon.
She doesn't insist she's right.

Her lanterns swing in the wind.
Her ex-husband visits, brings soup.
Her daughters do as they're told.

She sits up with mirror and comb.
She grips the bed rail in her sleep.
She speaks ashes to ashes.

8.

I visit Mother for another week. Will she be here
when I return next month? I can't hear the answer
above the engine noise of my heart. She reads

the blank wall of the guest room like a movie starring
herself. Shape-shifters drift by her door. Windstorms
mess the queen sheets. *Who unmade the duvet?* Her

mind is a layer cake rising on the idea of itself. Arms
linked at the elbows, we stand at the window, two women
intent on spying a sparrow perch, peck, and away.

I Am the Empty Nest

The first one flew away. Higher
education. The second stayed

in the nest. She wasn't ready.
Good, neither was I. Didn't last.

She grew up, fledged. If there
is a better metaphor, I don't know it,

haven't heard it. I am every cliché
in the book. I am home where

my heart is. I am time running out.
I am careful for what I wish.

I am what I eat. I am cake, shaped
in honour of the nest. I crack eggs,

separate whites, add one cup sugar,
pinch of salt, a little cornstarch.

Whip at high speed until thick peaks
rise. I heap the mess onto a metal

sheet. Sculpt with a spatula, create
an airy meringue. Bake an hour on

low, leave to cool in oven overnight.
Crusty brittle outside, creamy smooth

inside. I am every cloud with a silver
lining. My first and my last flock

to my table for pavlova often as they're
able, spoon cake garnished with lemon

curd, pitted red cherries, raspberries,
blackberries, kiwi slices, ripe peach.

My sweet grief, the one that comes 'n goes,
a thing with feathers.

Crimson Scarlet Cardinal Rose

Do I miss you, Little Red?
Do I miss counting the days between?
Do I miss the watchful wait?
Do I miss shopping for you?
Do I miss stocking your white supplies?
Do I miss your damp rose dot?
Do I miss your cardinal stain?
Do I miss the scrub and rinse?
Do I miss your crimson trace?
Do I miss the cramped room?
Do I miss the toss, the turn, the sleepless nights?
Do I miss our secret squat?
Do I miss the scalding bath?
Do I miss tablets, teas, head between my knees?
Do I miss the fisted clot?
Do I miss the scarlet bowl?
Do I miss you in bed with me for the day?
Do I miss the few pounds shed?
Do I miss you, Little Red?

Camel-Wool Coat

Today I want to pick up the phone and dial,
hear that click of connection tunnel my ear.
How fast the time, how slow. Your camel-wool
coat still hangs in my closet. A Friday, late
afternoon at home, remember?

It remains, your death, I mean, the event we never
turned inside out, the who said what when and how.
Silly, I know. Impossible, I know, I know. But talk,
gossip, was our hobby. Letters, your move to email

and best of all, eye to eye over a cup of coffee after
a day spent shopping for fabric to replace the thin
brown lining of your coat. Pockets of conversation,
fully dressed events discussed like seamstresses
hunched over their machines.

So much stillness now. My phone sits in its cradle,
lost as a dropped glove. Yet I answer the silence, speak
the questions you ask down the line. Yes, you looked
like you had fallen asleep in the reading chair, hair

freshly washed and coloured chestnut, jeans clean,
pressed, your blue sweater unwrinkled as your powdered
chin. How long? I sat with you until night fell and two
men in black suits arrived from the funeral home.

Together we draped a white sheet, moved your body
to a stretcher. And then I walked. I walked at your side
to the front door and out to the driveway where a long
black car sat idling. But you didn't speak last-minute
instructions, didn't tell me when I'd see you next,

didn't wave as I stood on the concrete steps, not
knowing what to do with my hands or my feet or my
mouth as the red tail lights signalled through the darkness,
blinked a right turn, and you were gone.

Can't Get the Smell of Smoke Out of My Hair

I'm leaping flames, throwing doors open
in the house where I was born. Where
are you? I need to model a dress before
the dream overheats because what I'm
wearing once belonged to Emily Dickinson.
We're the same size, Emily and I.

Oh Mother, the most famous day dress
in America is a nightgown that might burst
bright at any moment. The living room?
You died the first day of April. Over time,
I've come to think it's funny. Not dying,
but how the living room's propaganda got
the last laugh on all of us.

If you hadn't died two hours before my train
arrived, if your heart hadn't braked, we'd
have dined together, chicken stew, a fruity
Chardonnay, licked our lips. You were sick
but we liked to pretend.

This is the trouble with dreams and dying,
the dream roams from dark to light while the
dying go dark. Two separate piles of laundry.

You sewed *Vogue* patterns, taught me
how to model unfinished dresses, walk the long
hallway off the kitchen. Midpoint turn, pose,
while you pinned the hem, shortened a sleeve.

Where are you? I have no one to show and bellow
my dream, twelve buttons ablaze, lace cuffs
flaming, Emily's charcoal pencil a spark in the
patch pocket at my right hip.

You told me, you told me, *Never play with fire.*
It wasn't me, it was Emily. Where oh where
are you? I'm getting closer, braver, am I hot?

Keeping Mum

I return to pack your closet, a private room once
kingdom to a child, walls lined with treasure, hexagon
hat boxes, shoe boxes, pastel dresses, silk robes and
beaded gowns, hems caressing the top of my head
as I crawl deep, while you count, *Eight, nine, ten.*

Did you know where I hid? It was a game that won
you silence, a second cup, a few more pages.

Ready or not, I'm here to collect a lifetime of sweaters
hanging slump-shouldered, double-knit pantsuits
dry-cleaned and plastic-veiled, cotton dresses
embroidered in *des colores,* bright as your wish for
one more Mexican winter.

Come find me, bent below a naked yellow light,
my arm stemmed through the fallen sleeve of your
navy-blue housecoat, my feet crushing the backs
of your best black shoes.

Left Behind

The double bed is barely big enough for two yet she's the dog
and we are husband and wife pushed to the edge. We upgrade
to queen. She thanks us by moping in the rooms abandoned
by the teenagers who left her behind. I resort to chicken livers
sautéed in goose fat, bake biscuits studded with deer sausage,
haul water from glacial springs only to chase her wild escapes
across traffic and down into wooded ravines.

I was never so lean, so muscled, so generous with beef bones,
tennis balls, Italian leather slippers, the wool socks on my feet.
No task too great, too humble. I clip her nails, swab her ears,
brush and comb the reason I rise every day with the sun, let
my husband sleep.

She's the boundless dig to the depths of my heart that one day
pounds against an unfamiliar silence. *Where is she?* Sleep had
become her favourite game, yet her side of the bed is cold as
breakfast. *Where is she?* I whistle, call, pace every room in the
house, search every couch, every pillow, the stepping stones
that reach like an arm through the back garden, for there she is
and here I am, on my knees in the damp, grassy shade, lifting
a paw, begging.

Two-Minute Eulogy

My stepmother agreed to read
a psalm. Green pastures, quiet

waters, the darkest valley.
The reverend suggested hymns,

prayer, asked who would deliver
the eulogy for my father. She gave

me twenty minutes. I wrote, timed
my lines, practised alone out loud,

listened to my daughters rehearse
verses from a book they see once

a year. If we attend. My sister insisted
she couldn't speak without sobbing.

We each did as bid. I spoke in honour
of the man who taught me never cheat,

never lie. In truth, I could have left
eighteen minutes on the dais, donated

time to the reverend for more prayer,
a third verse. I needed only enough

breath that morning to stand, face
the congregation in my father's church

to say he lathered before he shaved,
smelled like fresh snow and mint

toothpaste. His *rise and shine* was my
daily weather. He mashed my boiled

potatoes with the back of his fork,
passed the butter. He caused me into

something. I mean, I was really
something in his eyes. My sister, too.

The Bitter End

I accepted their sympathies, agreed my father
was a good man. Yes, may he rest in peace.
May I? Not yet. A few guests lingered, sipped
coffee. I stayed, played host. My husband

left the visitation to drive my stepmother five
blocks to the townhouse replete with Dad's
shirts, shoes, slippers, butterscotch toffees
in a candy dish. The two of them were a pair

of snowbirds, flew south every winter. Except
his last. My sister, her face pale as skim milk,
slipped out earlier. She hadn't slept the night
before. My daughters followed, dutiful, done in

from greeting, hugging, listening to friends,
relatives. The bones in my feet ached. My eyeballs
felt baked in their orbits. *Thank you, thank you
so much for coming.* Soon my husband would return

for me in the rental car, warm leather seats, heater
blowing. Soon I'd join my own family, soon
as this last guest finished a story lost on me, my focus
overcome by the sickly sweet smell of dead flowers

wilting in vases, an off-centre centrepiece, faint
white lilies, limp yellow roses set on a serving table,
the linen pocked with coffee stains, dirty spoons,
half-eaten tarts, oatmeal cookie crumbs, lukewarm

mayonnaise dip, carrot sticks dried at the ends
and curled like beckoning fingertips. I slid down
onto the nearest chair. An elderly man with brown
stumps for teeth pumped my hand. I don't recall

if I thanked him, wished him well. My tongue dry,
my ears deaf to the last voices in the tilted room
except the pitch of one. Her voice. My late mother
cremated almost two years earlier, consumed by fire,

reduced to bone-grey scattered ashes, come to pay
her final respects. *Your father was a horse's ass.*
That bitter taste in the dregs of coffee someone
poured from a metal urn.

Red Plaid Blanket

I didn't have the energy to decorate a tree that Christmas
but I relented, stood a balsam fir in the living room for
the adults who were once my little kids. Faced the season,
our first without Papa. A new year arriving in twelve days.
I can do anything for twelve days.

January One: I stripped away tinsel, unhooked flightless
birds, glass balls, mute bells, the angel whose halo
is forever askew. And then? I parted the tinder-dry branches
at mid-height, gripped the trunk with both hands, tipped
the timber over and down onto the red plaid blanket my father
always packed in the trunk of his car. Needles netted my hair.
Medicinal smell of resin. My fingers, both palms, gummed
with pine sap.

The frozen air stunned my breath as I opened the front door.
I dipped my chin, turned and stepped back inside to finish
the job. Bent my knees, my back, wrapped both arms around
the dead tree, lifted and dragged its weight through
the heart of my home, into bitter cold winter.

Black Umbrella

Now you're gone I can't stop the rain in my dreams
now you're gone it rains and rains.

An Early Evening Hour Inside Out

All My Questions Kneel Down

1.

How my pulse quicks to the sound of your voice, beloved,
in from away. No bells, no knock, no warning, just the cool
rush of wind as you come in. Back of my knees. I turn,
and in the turning, how wide open the door. A window
inside adore. How your long legs sweep across and into.
All for me. How greedy, how selfish. How giddy-up, get
along little heart. In from away. How you surprise. Every
time. How once the door was half closed but now it's wide
open. To all of you. Leaf stemmed to your hatband. Light
slicing through thin green leaf. How you flutter me in deep
embrace. How we stand locked inside our front door.

2.

Where the February sky holds a Snow Moon full as love
in the making. Then all my questions kneel down. Kneel
with arms crossed. Blushed faces turned to heaven.
Where there is love. I cannot best this dark winter night
made bright: lunar light in the window, snow falling
as we fall asleep.

3.

When your body contorts the bedsheets as you flail,
your wings in nightmare fright. I wonder: do I love
this creature. When once I knew a woman who loved
a bear because he was savage and gentle, both. Me,
I have known you only as a gentle man during the long
length of our marriage, yet you navigate two worlds
while I have only this one. When you leave me. When
loneliness thrashes against its own cave.

4.
Who sails the black lake as gulls scissor the atmosphere.
I focus my binoculars, ignore the squawk. Walk. My father
was a weekend sailor. Is it him I spy in a craft rigged
with main sail and jib. Him beyond and now returned on the
crest. If the answer is yes, if the answer is no, do I drop my
extra set of eyes and swim. Who plays these tricks. My father's
ashes buried not far from shore yet these eyes reach for one
last look. Look: that's me in the far boat, me as first mate,
a rope pulled tight, muscles alert to the captain's command.
Who calls above the call of wind and feathers.

5.
The quarrel rises. What we do not touch but accept. What
desperate arrangements we make in our house. Your long
hours, my few minutes with pen and paper. We argue, pace.
Another storm, followed by radio waves. A song about the
moon and a river. A tune I heard my parents play on the hi-fi
in their living room. Thirty-three revolutions per minute.
Stocking feet on gold wall-to-wall carpet. Couples spin apart,
grow apart. What you whisper to me as we stand and sway.
We can be that long-playing record. What now.

6.
Why we stand on the patio of a southern holiday house as
talcum-white birds land in the singular. Until a gathering of
question marks. Necks bent, wings folded against answers
fished from a pond. A pond with a fountain that cascades until
sunset when a mechanical clock shuts down the sound of rain.
Why we need to know. Not the answers, but the true name.
Egrets. Why good fortune laughs on the rhyme. A flock of
regrets. We might have been. Had you not. But you did.
And in the asking, I said yes.

Latitude

I stand behind an upholstered armchair where my friend
sits cradling the guest of honour, a baby snuggled in a
black sleeper patterned with bright yellow stars. Coos
flutter the room as Star Baby is passed from woman to
woman to woman like a platter of mooncakes.

Margot's arms give him up and over to Jane, who stands
to rock Star Baby. I catch the smell of sour, undigested
milk. What will I do if Jane offers me the bundle of
cotton? My arms stiffen at the elbows. I step back from
the chair, away from Laura, Barb, and Carol so that no
one assumes I'm in line, waiting my turn to hold Liling's baby.

I move into Cathy's dining room where a cut-glass vase
of impossible pink roses anchors the middle of the table.
Impossible because the stems began as hothouse roots
potted south of the equator. Now they're in Saskatoon,
one dozen blooms decorating a room in a house built
for winters at Latitude 52.

The flowers for beautiful Liling are a gift from all of us,
mothers of grown-up children. Empty nesters, a descriptor,
a syndrome, a sorrow that spreads like the flu passing through
a crowded room.

I wonder how women in China honour new babies but
the question feels like a chore the instant it forms. I'd have
to walk back into the living room, arrange my face, find
a chair, speak, listen, converse.

I survey the table. Cathy has set out goat cheese and rice
crackers, bowls of strawberries tossed with pineapple chunks,
blueberries no bigger than the tip of a baby's thumb, salted
cashews, dried apricots, apple slices, mango, tiny quiches,
cake (warm ginger-pear), china plates, napkins, forks, spoons,
coffee. I lift, pour.

I recall a story about a woman whose job with a florist
was to trim rose stems. Something about a baby. No,
it was the thorns; they lay on the paper like lost baby teeth.
I set down my cup, raise my hand to my heart until I feel
a pulse beat its way through layers of bra, camisole,
turtleneck sweater: *Hold the baby.*

What I want to hold in my arms is my coat. I need my coat.
Where? The guest room, the double bed. I seize a confusion
of black nylon zippered fronts, backs, sleeves, hoods trimmed
with fake fur, fox fur, coyote. I clutch and fumble with a side
pocket, my too many keys, will myself to say goodbye to the
new mother, move in the direction of Liling's full-moon face
until I find those deep black eyes. How they track her baby's
orbit with animal intention. *Congratulations again, Liling.*
Such a busy day, must run. Outside to my car and into the din
of traffic, blurred lines, the cropped rear-view of my babies,
my breasts engorged with phantom pain for the suck lamented,
our primal pull.

That First Killing Frost of the Season
for Cathy, in memoriam

My cell phone pinged with news of your death
the same moment my eyes fell on the blackened leaves

of a basil plant, victim to the season's first frost.
I was in the garden, pulling old bedsheets from the heads

of red geraniums, covers I'd set the night before, but in my
haste to protect potted annuals from a chill that always

claims its kill, I'd overlooked the luscious green herb
at the foot of the garden. How could I? How could you?

I'd been hoping against science for your luminous brain
to stop bleeding, remap itself. I'd been hoping against

reason for an endless summer. I'd been hoping against
hope for more time. What to do? What to do? I kneeled

down in the dirt beside the basil plant, fingered slack leaves
turned black and silky-soft as earlobes, inhaled the morning's

cold air to jump-start my logic. Was I truly grieving you
and a common herb in the same heartbeat? I touched my lips

to still my pain when a pungent scent shot me back to the
hundreds of cookouts, picnics, potlucks, recipes shared

for tomato salads studded with creamy mozzarella and basil,
savoury breads laced with basil, soup seasoned with oily-rich

swirls of basil. My friend, the text arrived with the certainty of
frost. Soon the earth will freeze and harden. For now,

during these thin hours of disbelief, I conjure your spirit
crossing that cold starry night under watch of an ancient herb,

clusters of cupped leaves dying to bid you godspeed.

An Early Evening Hour Inside Out

If you quicken your pace and walk in step along the park
path, you in a brown wool jacket, your daughter in denim,
if you inhale the raw late-afternoon air, lean into her voice,

you might accept the hollow longing born three decades ago,
the clamp and cut under medical glare, that moment her life
moved outside without you. If you ask yourself what's the

bloody problem, why the old ache, is this not what you
wanted, has she not gone forward, built her own big life, and
returned to live nearby? Yes and yes and yes and. You want

more. Always more. Yet here she is, a young woman running
errands on a hectic day off, a woman who sends a text to her
mother—*I'm nearby do you have time for a visit while my car*

gets fixed?—you, chosen to share the hour before the garage
closes, the hour of dusk, *vespers*, a word that recurs
unexpected as warmth in the weakening autumn light, the

fading botanical scent of hair strayed from a knitted toque
topped with a nodding pompom, one hour set aside, enough
for you to walk beside the life you carried until she crowned.

If you stop looking back over your shoulder, if you accept
that you miss her even while she's with you, if you don't look
ahead, you will honour all the bright and dark hours required

for a daughter to reach the dirt footpath eroded over time by
animals and humans, a path of desire cut across this green
inner-city park, you and your daughter walking the way

women have walked and talked and ached forever, the evening's early hour, the massive dog she rescued as a pup straining its leather lead.

Bus #12, Saskatoon to Amsterdam

I've been knitting this dream since her first kiss
to the centre of my wrinkled forehead, when I weighed
no more than a bushel of feathers. My newborn skin
smelled like her pain had been worth the price of
my arrival.

The price I paid was exact fare, dropped into a metal
canister. *Dank u wel,* I said to the bus driver. I was
on my way to Amsterdam from a city on the prairies
where I learned the word *dun.* As in the dun-coloured
fields.

I picked a window seat, pretended the green backpack
balanced on my lap was a toddler in a snowsuit amused
by cars, elm trees, grey scarves scudding by. I'd packed
with care, packed interchangeable pieces of black wash-
and-wear so I'd always look clean, blend with the other
tourists.

The bus lifted off.

We soon reached an altitude where anything was possible.

A woman with dun-coloured hair same as my own moved
from her single seat to the empty bench across from me.
She wore a white terry-cloth housecoat with a shawl collar,
carried a newborn lamb tucked under one arm like a sack
of sugar. Our knees touched. We were as close as mother
and daughter. The lamb smelled of baby shampoo.

She leaned in closer, warned me, *Don't gawk at the passenger across the aisle with wavy black hair because that's Anne Frank, the girl who wrote Dear Kitty, Dear Kitty, Dear Kitty, in the pages of a red plaid diary.* I had a bad habit as a child. I stared at people when I rode the bus downtown with my mother. I looked away before Anne caught me. Too late.

Anne asked if the seat beside me was reserved. I leaned my shoulder against the window, made extra room. Anne wished to know the name of the lamb, but when my mother said *Claude,* Anne heard *cloud,* and so gathered a gentle rain inside the bus where we huddled to protect little Claude, a sweet creature we passed from my mother to Anne, who pressed her ear against lamb's small chest before handing him up and over the head of Vincent van Gogh, who watched me watching him from a scene within a self-portrait. Yet he, too, extended his long arms, offered little lamb to a Japanese pianist unable to lift his eyes from a Russian cellist, her plunging beaded neckline. He forgot himself, and kissed wee Claude smack on the nose.

We laughed, all of us, including the jolly fellows at the rear of the bus, a dark blond trio of cheese farmers. They blushed the same shade as their moist red lips.

The Modern Woman's Guide to Aging

Friends
Make pals with Grace. She's the woman
who pierces flesh for a living,
marinates snap beans in whisky
and if you're lucky, and you are, she'll invite
you fishing, silver hook,
long line, the lake a mirror
where you fall
in love
      with yourself.

Wardrobe
Go pigeon and call yourself
rock dove. Dress top to tail
in slate-grey, flaunt
style with twin black stripes
where your wings fold,
toss an iridescent green scarf
around your neck, pink
socks for spark,
boots.

Health
There are days when your bones complain
and too many people ask too many questions.

No need to confess that it wasn't the flu
that sent you back to bed. It was the sad stones
in your heart that simply ran out of room.

Go for a walk, wear your hat with the feather,
relinquish your sorrows to the prairie.

Diet
Don't.

Finances
Every wrinkle
every grey hair
every soft fold
every double chin
every varicose vein
every bunion
every mole
every dry knuckle
every capped tooth
every back pain
every migraine
speaks in honour of
your rich life.

Name in the Dark

Ester tried to leap the cabin balcony, afraid
of her daughter Laura in the kitchen peeling
carrots with a knife. Laura's blue eyes are lost
to Ester, along with three grandchildren, all
the constellations Ester identified for the friends
she treated like family on summer nights
at the lake, blankets draped over our bare legs,
necks craned skyward, the scent of pine and spruce
mixed with the day's catch. Now Laura visits
her widowed mother in a home. Windows don't
open. Staff wear uniforms in cartoon prints.
Mickey, Minnie, Pluto.

It's hard to be human, says Laura. Friends for
over forty years, we hug one another in the hall
outside of Ester's room, the door closed. I don't
know what to say except *thanks.* Thanks for
sharing her mother, thanks for the invitation
to say farewell to a woman who loved me like
a daughter.

Let Laura turn the lock in the door.
Let her step from her thin brown leather sandals.
Let her lie abed, child and mother.
Let there be rest and last breath.
Let every constellation hold Ester's name in the dark.

Primary Colours
after Alex Dimitrov

I love my dearest without thinking I love him,
plus all the days I don't but I do.
I love blue.
I love the song.
I love the needle, the thread, the button.
I love my faded jeans.
I love his long legs.
I love the balletic balance of snow on a wire fence.
I love the undrunk woman on the West Coast
who remade herself sober.
I love my clear head.
I love hikes along the South Saskatchewan River shore
in spring, massive ice sheets heaving like wrecked yachts.
I love the broken among us.
I love my mother's cursive hand.
I love the homes my daughters own, nearby.
I love the nearby.
I love the monikers for my City of Bridges, Magic City,
Paris of the Prairies.
I love the back of my troubles.
I love the white shirts my father wore most of his life.
I love sparrows.
I love yellow.
I love the driver who yields to a stop while I cross.
I love black rubber boots with thick orange soles.
I love eggs, scrambled, poached, flipped.
I love the word *quotidian* but seldom used it until
the pandemic returned the everyday to my life.
I love buttered toast.

I love his housecoat and mine hooked slack from the back
of the bedroom door.
I love the ritual of morning.
I love the dark coffee he brews in the stainless-steel
six-cup pot.
I love the sweet dust that sugar cubes shed in the slide-out
cardboard box.
I love sweaters that skim my bum.
I love the insistence of dandelions.
I love a ripe Anjou pear cut and forked with a fruit knife.
I love red.
I love the name Ruby.
I love pencils.
I love willow trees.
I love deep, functional pockets.
I love birds' nests.
I love my canoe.
I love the Brontë sisters.
I love my only sister, only.
I love dried chamomile flowers, the scent they release
under water boiled for late-night tea.
I love the room upstairs in our house where twin skylights
let the light.
I love reading. Everything.
I love all twenty-six letters.
I love the spoon more than the fork but not as much
as the knife.
I love rock, paper, scissors.
I love my local bakery, the wood fire, brick oven,
one rye loaf sliced for pickup every Friday.
I love white linen on a picnic table.

I love wool socks.
I love my tent, the vestibule, zipper, womb.
I love moisture in the air.
I love Ali MacGraw's nostrils.
I love handkerchiefs.
I love the letters he wrote to me and I wrote to him,
though I will never open them again because the people
inside are so young.
I love climbing into bed at night while he reads naked.
I love the woman at the gym who arrives with her walker
and tries and tries and tries.
I love molt, as in the snake molts its skin.
I love rhubarb's raw red knuckle thrusting up
from under.
I love tossing the salad.

Notes

The introductory epigraph is taken from "Prairie Poem," by Margaret Avison, published in volume three of *Always Now* (Porcupine's Quill, 2003). Used by permission of the executor of the estate, Joan Eichner, and the publisher.

The first set of italicized lines in "Ferus" are from Rainer Maria Rilke's poem "The Dark Hours of My Being," published in *Rilke's Book of Hours: Love Poems to God,* translated by Anita Barrows and Joanna Macy (The Berkley Publishing Group, 1996). The later italicized lines are from "Messenger" in *The View from Castle Rock* by Alice Munro (McClelland & Stewart, 2006). Used by permission of the publishers.

"The Heart Wants" takes its title from a letter Emily Dickinson wrote in 1862 to her friend Mary Bowles. She wrote, "The heart wants it wants—or else it does not care." The letter is found in *The Letters of Emily Dickinson,* edited by Thomas H. Johnson; associate editor, Theodora Ward (The Belknap Press of Harvard University Press, 1986). Used by permission of the publisher.

In "Latitude," the phrase "they lay on the paper like lost baby teeth" is from Mary Gaitskill's short story "Heaven" in *Bad Behavior* (Vintage Books, 1989). Used by permission of the publisher.

The italicized lines in "Inside the Domestic Triangle" indicate the titles of paintings by Mary Pratt, as well as commentary from her book, *A Personal Calligraphy* (Goose Lane Editions, 2000). Used by permission of the publisher.

The last line in "I Am the Empty Nest" is from "314 'Hope' is the thing with feathers," published in *The Poems of Emily Dickinson: Variorum Edition,* edited by Ralph W. Franklin (The Belknap Press of Harvard University Press, 1998). Used by permission of the publisher.

"The Modern Woman's Guide to Aging" echoes lines by two

Saskatchewan poets: "who pierces / flesh for a living snaps" appeared in Belinda Betker's "Pierce" in *Phrases* (Coteau Books, 2019); "it wasn't the flu / the sad stones in my heart simply ran out of room" appeared in Barbara Langhorst's *Restless White Fields* (NeWest Press, 2012). Used by permission of the authors.

Acknowledgements

I thank the Canada Council for the Arts and the Saskatoon Public Library for support during my term as the library's 2017-2018 Writer in Residence. The residency provided me with time to finish many of these poems. The manuscript later won the City of Regina Writing Award (2018) and the John V. Hicks Long Manuscript Award (2018), sponsored by the Saskatchewan Writers' Guild.

An earlier version of "On the Horizon" was published as the chapbook *Start with the Answer* after winning the 2009 gritLIT poetry competition. Other poems were previously published or anthologized in *Grain, The Maple Leaf Rag V: An Anthology of Poetic Writings, Prairie Fire, Line Dance: An Anthology of Poetry, untethered, Where the Nights Are Twice as Long: Love Letters of Canadian Poets, Wilf Perreault: In the alley/Dans la ruelle, Hamilton Arts & Letters*, and *CBC Books*. Thank you to the editors.

Bouquets to the publishing team at Turnstone Press who said yes to the manuscript in its early stage despite the rough edges. Much gratitude to editor Di Brandt for her insightful questions and comments.

Deep thanks to my family and friends, those who appear in these pages and those who cheered from the margins. Thanks especially to Randy, who once ran to meet me outside the train station in Lyon, France carrying a black umbrella in the pouring rain.

Katherine Lawrence is the author of three poetry collections and a verse novel. Originally from Hamilton, she lived in Ottawa and Whitehorse before moving to the traditional lands of the Cree, Saulteaux, Dene, Dakota, Lakota, Nakota, and Métis nations, in Saskatoon, Saskatchewan. Her work has been published in many Canadian journals, and has won several awards, including a Saskatchewan Book Award for *Ring Finger, Left Hand* and the Moonbeam Award in Children's Poetry for *Stay*. From 2017 to 2018, Katherine served as Writer in Residence for the Saskatoon Public Library. She holds an MFA in Writing from the University of Saskatchewan. She is the mother of two daughters.

www.Katherinelawrence.net